100% UNOFFICIAL
FORTNITE
ANNUAL 2023

CONTENTS

100%
UNOFFICIAL

100%
UNOFFICIAL

First published in Great Britain 2022 by
100% Unofficial, a part of Farshore
An imprint of HarperCollins*Publishers*
1 London Bridge Street, London SE1 9GF
www.farshore.co.uk

HarperCollins*Publishers*
1st Floor, Watermarque Building, Ringsend Road
Dublin 4, Ireland

Written by Kevin Pettman
Illustrated by Matt Burgess

This book is an original creation by Farshore
© 2022 HarperCollinsPublishers Limited

ISBN 978 0 0085 0771 8
Printed in Romania

3

ONLINE SAFETY FOR YOUNGER FANS

Spending time online is great fun! Here are a few simple rules to help younger fans stay safe and
keep the internet a great place to spend time:

- Never give out your real name – don't use it as your username.
- Never give out any of your personal details.
- Never tell anybody which school you go to or how old you are.
- Never tell anybody your password except a parent or a guardian.
- Be aware that you must be 13 or over to create an account on many sites.
Always check the site policy and ask a parent or guardian for permission before registering.
- Always tell a parent or guardian if something is worrying you.

Stay safe online. Any website addresses listed in this book are correct at the time of going to print.
However, Farshore is not responsible for content hosted by third parties. Please be aware that online
content can be subject to change and websites can contain content that is unsuitable for children.
We advise that all children are supervised when using the internet.

FORTNITE FOREVER

Welcome to the world's most awesome gaming experience! Fortnite Battle Royale just keeps on bossing it, with new themes, locations, events and characters season after season and year after year. It's no surprise that millions of gamers just like you keep dropping on the island for an exciting mix of action and quests.

Your 100% Unofficial Fortnite Annual 2023 is rammed with all the essential intel you need. From reliving Chapter 2's most memorable moments to elite level tips and tactics, weapon guides, special skins, epic items and so much more. Whether you like to play as a solo star or team up with your favourite squad, get ready to discover all the best bits that make Fortnite Battle Royale the ultimate adventure!

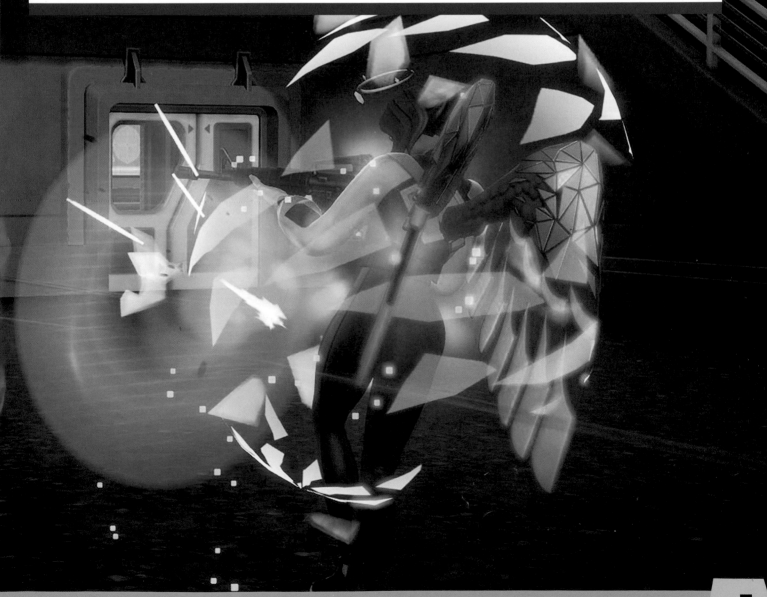

THE STORY OF CHAPTER 2

Chapter 2 has already uncovered a huge range of storylines and talking points, from giant cubes and portals to alien invasions, wild animals and bounty hunters.

ANIMAL INSTINCT

There was a time when the closest you came to a wild animal on the island was when a player wore the Bunny Brawler oufit, but that all changed in Chapter 2 Season 6. Creatures such as boars, wolves, chickens and frogs cropped up around the island. The beasts had a few uses, including dropping meat when you defeated them, but more imporantly, you could tame them so they would fight by your side.

ALIEN INVASION

Fortnite really did become an out-of-this-world experience in Season 7! Unwelcome aliens attacked the island from the skies and forced a fight-back from Doctor Slone and the secretive organisation, the Imagined Order. The invasion led to all sorts of new weapons, items, tech, creatures and characters arriving, with players at the forefront of a battle to take back control of their beloved island from the visitors.

CUBE CHAOS

The most momentous change to the Season 8 map was the sudden appearance of the Cubes. These mysterious objects had shown up in various forms over the years, the most notable being the island-trotting Kevin, who appeared in Chapter 1. This time their crash-landing from the Mothership opened a portal route to the ever-changing Sideways zone.

SCARY SIGHT

As battlers entered the Sideways zone, they were greeted by monolithic Cube monsters, who became seriously scary opponents at the start of Chapter 2 Season 8. It was worth the risk to take them down, though, as they had the chance to drop Sideways weapons and monster parts for crafting upgrades when they were defeated.

THE HUNT IS ON

Don't forget that Chapter 2 also witnessed the arrival of NPCs (non-player characters) that you could hunt down or complete quests for. Some of the faves included Mancake, Mave, Reese and Lexa. Some could be hired, in exchange for bars earned by doing bounties, and then shadow you to beef up your protection.

Chapter 2 has already uncovered a huge range of storylines and talking points, from giant cubes and portals to alien invasions, wild animals and bounty hunters.

DOCTOR, DOCTOR

If you ventured over to the Corny Complex, you'd find Doctor Slone lurking somewhere. This boss was a complex character to deal with indeed! However, she was the only route to obtaining the mythic Slone pulse rifle, but you had to watch out for the two clone guards that flanked her.

DROP OFF

Chapter 2 introduced the ability to collect some special weapons from bosses and NPCs, either through elimination or purchasing with bars. During the alien invasion season, for example, Abstrakt could offer you the marksman six shooter, Zyg and Choppy had their mythic ray gun and Riot could reward you with the storm scout sniper rifle. Cool!

CRAFTY MOVES

The ability to craft your own weapons, rather than looting them, arrived in Chapter 2 Season 6, which was labelled as the Primal season. It started when animal bones arrived as an item, which you then used to build Primal weapons. The following season, the addition of nuts and bolts meant serious crafting upgrades were on offer – for example, an assault rifle could be transformed into a burst variant and a pump shottie could be lovingly crafted into a lever action version of the same rarity.

LIFT OFF

Being levitated off the ground by a hovering abductor was a scary feeling the first time it happened. That was until you realised it transported you to the mothership, where you could stock up on more powerful weapons before returning to the island. On board the mothership, the aim was to collect vault and time orbs, which respectively unlocked high-level vaults and increased the time you had before the abductors dropped you back to Earth.

BIG DECISIONS

Donation boards sprang up around the island during Season 8, as a way to allow gamers to decide when and where certain features and items could appear. You could vote by dropping your hard-earned bars at the donation board in order to choose your preferred feature. The first donation board-dictated feature to appear was a turret station at Boney Burbs. What a blast!

FRESH FASHION

Where would Fortnite be without all of the outrageous outfits, sick skins and lethal looks it lets you create on a daily basis? Eye-catching gear pops up in the item shop or as part of the Battle Pass throughout a season. Sunny, Human Bill and Guernsey are memorable skins from the last year, as well as collaborations with the likes of Superman and Rick Sanchez.

TOP DISCOVERY

Getting to grips with your favourite minigame or Fortnite experience was made much easier during Chapter 2. The new Discovery tab gives you a quick and easy route to the type of stuff you love, which may be co-op or adventure-style games, as well as the ability to 'favourite' it with the heart symbol. The My Library tab has a helpful selection of your recently played games.

DISCOVER   MY LIBRARY   CREATE   ISLAND CODE

CREATOR - Epic Games

ONE SHOT

XP | EPIC BY EPIC | DUOS | 100 MAX PLAYERS

Low Health! Low Gravity! Snipers Only! Jump, Aim, and Shoot your way to the Victory Royale!

TRENDING

BY EPIC

BY EPIC

WILD TIMES

Kicking off in Chapter 2 Season 6, Wild Weeks are seven-day events that rip up the Royale rulebook and change a fundamental part of the gameplay. They have been a big hit with the community and often see items removed from the vault, as well as changing the spawn rates of items currently out of the vault. The debut Wild Week had a fire theme, while flying, fishing and stealth have also had their weeks to shine.

CELEB SPOTTING

The planet's most famous faces have always flocked to Fortnite and Season 2 was no different! Sport stars are always keen to get on the screen, and the likes of Harry Kane, Neymar and LeBron James have all joined the popular Icon Series. If you're a music fan, then Party Royale is the place to be – Ariana Grande totally rocked it during the Rift Tour in Chapter 7!

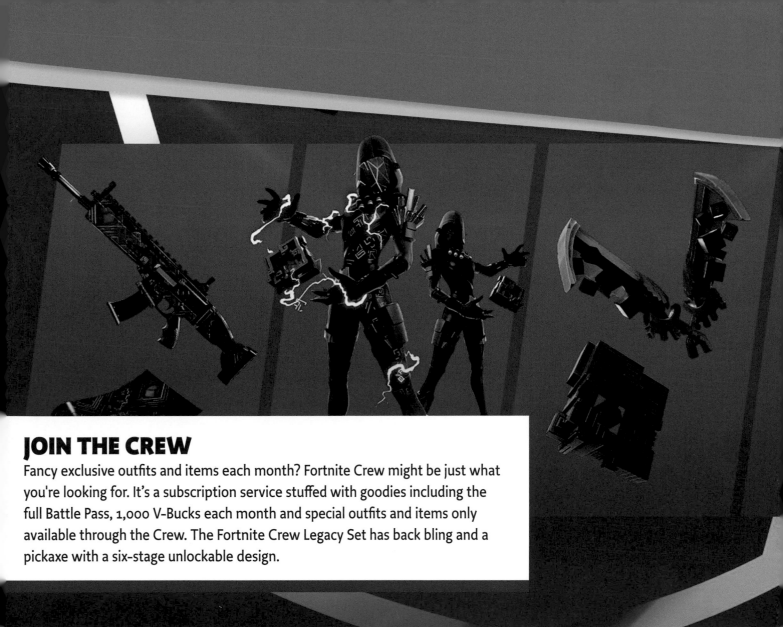

JOIN THE CREW

Fancy exclusive outfits and items each month? Fortnite Crew might be just what you're looking for. It's a subscription service stuffed with goodies including the full Battle Pass, 1,000 V-Bucks each month and special outfits and items only available through the Crew. The Fortnite Crew Legacy Set has back bling and a pickaxe with a six-stage unlockable design.

COMPETITION TIME

Competitive action keeps pro-level players, and others on a quest to improve their skills, at the top of their powers. This is where things get big-time sweaty, and events such as Epic Games' own Fortnite Champion Series (FNCS) regularly had a $3 million prize pool each season through 2021 and 2022! DreamHack, Cash Cup and Hype Cup are other tournaments that attract the best of Battle Royale.

ESSENTIAL INFO

Never fall into the trap of thinking you know it all! Get the basics covered and then build on your expertise – this speedy guide keeps you on the right track.

MATS MATTER

It's pretty much impossible to claim a Victory Royale or even get a whiff of the endgame without being able to build, and you won't build anything without a stash of materials, more commonly known as 'mats'. Wood, stone and metal – in that order – are your priority. You can use your pickaxe to harvest almost anything you can see in the game into one of these mats, then you can use those resources to build protective structures in seconds and get the high ground on the opposition.

BUILD BETTER

While your building techniques must be practised over time - Creative mode is a great place to experiment with this and improve your speed - there are four main areas to master. These are walls, ramps, floors and roofs. If you can perfectly place down each of these items, you'll soon be able to fend off enemy attacks from any direction and go deeper into the battle. Learning to edit your builds is another key step.

Land where you know you'll have good access to materials and a decent chance of getting a starter weapon. Going without resources and being unarmed for too long is a huge mistake.

WHICH WEAPON?

Confused by all the types and rarities of weapons in Fortnite? That's normal for newbies, but just remember that for short and mid-range combat you'll want a machine gun or shotgun, with rifles and most explosives suited to longer-range shootouts. Mythic and legendary weapons are the most powerful variants, but the green and blue auras of uncommon and rare guns should get you through the early stages of the game.

COUNT CORRECTLY

In a regular Battle Royale, the aim is to be the last player remaining. That's the only way Victory Royale will be achieved by you or your squad. The number of eliminations you make is not important, because technically you can win with just one final kill right at the end! Wiping out your enemies and racking up kills is defo impressive, but it's not essential and Fortnite calls on a range of combat tactics.

THRIVE AND SURVIVE

Having a decent stock of weapons is only the first step to achieving the elusive VR. You'll also need to keep an eye on your health and shields, shown as green and blue bars on the corner of your screen. The maximum value for both of these stats is 100 and if either drop anywhere near zero, then your survival is in serious danger. Forage food lying on the ground, loot medkits or shield potions and even do a spot of fishing to keep them all in tip-top shape as the battle progresses.

MOVE IT

There are two reasons why staying put and not stealthily switching from place to place is a very bad idea in Fortnite. Firstly, the enclosing storm is always decreasing the playing space, forcing you to move or take damage! Secondly, enemies will explore every nook and cranny for resources, so you'll probably be found anyway. Always keep moving and keep collecting weapons, mats and meds until the endgame draws near.

CHANGE GAME

Fortnite constantly evolves, which means you must keep up with the changes to the island on a constant basis. Even within Seasons, locations will develop and new characters will appear, often with new quests, items or some other boon that you can take advantage of. Make sure you visit all the different areas regularly to see what's new.

THE MAP

Navigate like a pro and know your way around the island like it's the back of your hand. While the map constantly changes, these named locations and landmarks have really stood out.

HOLLY HEDGES

Football pitch, alien-like zero gravity domes, Viking vessels ... a few small but special changes have happened in HH over in the far west of the island. Actually, during Chapter 2 Season 6, the place was branded Holly Hatchery when the alien biome showed up! Often a quiet spot to land and favoured by many new players.

BONEY BURBS

The words 'Tilted' and 'Towers' will mean something to you if you've been a Battle Royale fan for years. It was an appealing urban area in Chapter 1, which later became Neo Tilted and then Salty Towers after adopting aspects of Salty Springs. In Chapter 2 Season 6, Boney Burbs was another twist to this zone and had enough floor loot and chests to load you up in the early game. Hiding in the cornfields gave you cover to consume meds.

CORAL CASTLE

PLEASANT PA

BELIEVER BEACH

BONEY BURBS

...OLLY HEDGES

WEEPING WOODS

SLUDGY SWAMP

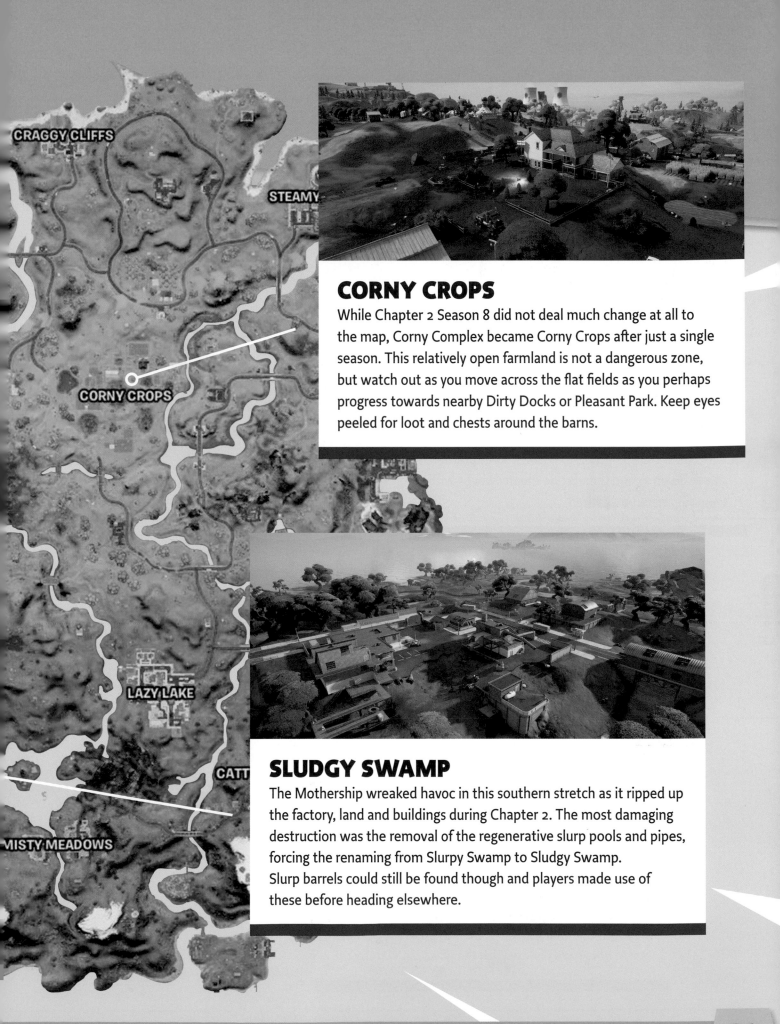

CRAGGY CLIFFS

STEAMY

CORNY CROPS

LAZY LAKE

CATT

MISTY MEADOWS

CORNY CROPS

While Chapter 2 Season 8 did not deal much change at all to the map, Corny Complex became Corny Crops after just a single season. This relatively open farmland is not a dangerous zone, but watch out as you move across the flat fields as you perhaps progress towards nearby Dirty Docks or Pleasant Park. Keep eyes peeled for loot and chests around the barns.

SLUDGY SWAMP

The Mothership wreaked havoc in this southern stretch as it ripped up the factory, land and buildings during Chapter 2. The most damaging destruction was the removal of the regenerative slurp pools and pipes, forcing the renaming from Slurpy Swamp to Sludgy Swamp.
Slurp barrels could still be found though and players made use of these before heading elsewhere.

THE MAP

BELIEVER BEACH

Renamed as Believer Beach in Chapter 2 Season 7 from Sweaty Sands, it lies in the north west of the island, immediately south of Coral Castle. It has always been a popular landing spot because of its mix of a tall building, small to medium-sized complexes and the cool pool to camp around. It was once home to plenty of alien features and with the water right next to it, see it as a spot to splash down at and then tackle enemy waves with the equipment you gather.

SHANTY TOWN

The slipstream wind tunnels that rocked up on the map in Chapter 2 Season 8 meant you could potentially reach different locations much more quickly and safely. Flying out west, past Weeping Woods and Sludgy Swamp, took you to the Shanty Town landmark. You need to look beyond the rundown handful of buildings and scope the place for weapons and materials – wood is in good supply here but AI bots have history with the place, so watch out!

CORAL CASTLE

PLEASANT P

BELIEVER BEACH

BONEY BURBS

HOLLY HEDGES

WEEPING WOODS

SLUDGY SWAMP

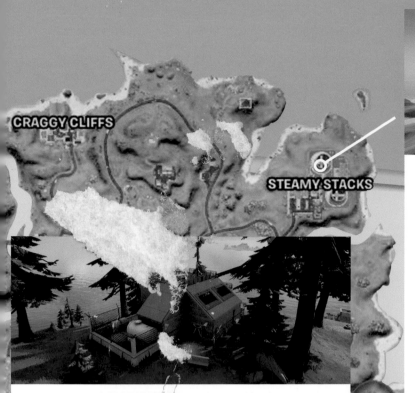

STEAMY STACKS

A difficult location to miss, with its two giant nuclear cooling towers and large-scale plant buildings belonging to Kevolution Energy. Steamy has tonnes of tarmac and concrete and in all honesty is a bit of an eyesore, but looks are deceptive as the place is packed with chests and loot. Don't forget to make a classy exit from this power-producing place by riding the zipline that heads south to Retail Row.

IO OUTPOSTS

The Imagined Order (IO) were dwarfed by the arrival of the Cubes in Season 8, but they still kept a presence in certain spots. A range of IO Outposts could be found in places such as Misty Meadows, Pleasant Park and Holly Hedges, and usually took the shape of a collection of small random buildings. They offered some chests, a speedy car and the chance to defeat an IO guard and collect a dropped weapon.

CAMP COD

Is this the best name ever for a Fortnite landmark? Tucked away on the south shores next to the water, which is a good job seeing as it's named after a fish, Camp Cod is a collection of odd scrap pieces from days gone by. One player's junk is another player's jewels, though, and there is always plenty of metal and weapons to pick up here. Be careful of the storm moving and be on your way pronto!

THE MAP

LOGJAM WOODWORKS

Max out your wood supplies by landing at this industrial spot to the west. The warehouse is a fab place to raid and then pick off opponents in the courtyard outside. In Chapter 2 Season 5, the Durr Burger restaurant suddenly smashed into the place – players loved raiding it for produce boxes that give your health a handy boost. It's well worth cruising by Logjam in the early to midgame phase.

FORT CRUMPET

A bit like Camp Cod, Fort Crumpet is posted out on the map's edges but has always been a great little landing spot. Head for the top of the tower and work down to the ground, or drop on the surrounding field and smash through the fort's ancient walls. 'Crumps' is not stuffed with loot but can be a prep zone before venturing to nearby Coral Castle.

WEEPING WOODS

Weeping Woods attracts lots of players, because whether you operate in solos or with your squad, the place has very good levels of chests, floor loot and ammo boxes. After plenty of visits you'll know the best loot route to take, which could mean hitting the tree-heavy central section first and then moving out to the surrounding buildings. Defo a solid spot for landing.

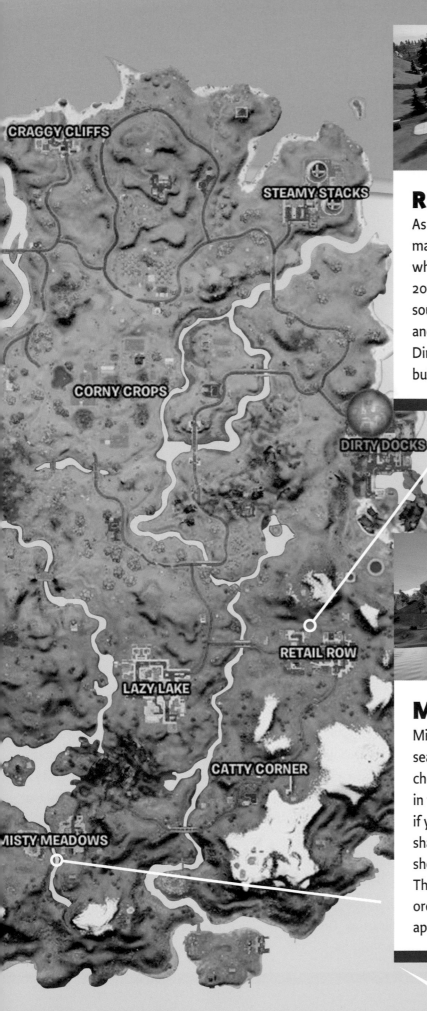

CRAGGY CLIFFS

STEAMY STACKS

CORNY CROPS

DIRTY DOCKS

RETAIL ROW

LAZY LAKE

CATTY CORNER

MISTY MEADOWS

RETAIL ROW

As the only original Fortnite location left on the map, Retail Row remains a firm fave with players who have been on the scene since way back in 2017. It can be a high traffic place to land, given its south east location that doesn't hug the coastline and the ease of rotating round to Lazy Lake or Dirty Docks. Move smartly through the shops and buildings and load up on all the lovely loot!

MISTY MEADOWS

Misty barely altered through the first eight seasons of Chapter 2 and had a significantly high chest spawn rate in Season 3 and 4. Take the road in from the west, but don't become an easy target if you cross the bridge on foot. Also, watch out for sharp snipers who could be plotting a long-range shot from the cover of the surrounding mountains. The colourful, pretty buildings give a sense of order, although Misty can be a place where danger appears with very little warning.

GET CREATIVE

Epic describes Creative mode as "made by you, played by you."
Find out all you need to know, plus some special codes to get you
involved with the ultimate community creations.

WHAT'S CREATIVE?

An online world, separate to
the main Battle Royale-focused
Fortnite island, where players
are free to create their own
unique build, game or experience.
Structures can be created as you
would in BR mode, or selected
and placed from a list of prefab
models, allowing you to quickly
make whole towns. You can even
populate the worlds with devices,
weapons and vehicles to make it
more interesting.

WHAT ARE CODES?

Creative codes let you find any
island that has ever been made.
Each saved island has a unique
12-digit code that will allow
access to it, so they can easily be
shared. Epic Games likes to shout
about the coolest creators and
releases lots of fantastic codes
so you can try a mix of maps.
We've got a few of our favourites
on the opposite page, as well as
throughout this book. Go ahead
and give them a try!

HOW DO I ACCESS?

Select the Creative tab from
the lobby to get to the main
Creative mode screen. You can
select a game you'd like to play
from a selection of community
favourites on the front page, and
a place to input codes, as well
as the option to start your own
Creative world. There are island
types and templates to choose.
There are plenty of tips and
tutorials available in the Creative
hub too.

FINEST'S REALISTIC 6570-5231-1418

Finest is the name of the creator behind this island adventure, which is a 2v2 set-up for a maximum of four players. The games are tight and quick, with a league ranking that displays each team's eliminations by player and damage dealt. It's highly addictive and perfect for practising and buffing up your shooting and building skills. Covering your partner's back and having eyes everywhere is essential.

PRISON BREAKOUT 6531-4403-0726

Creator Echo has busted out some top design skills in this jailbreak setup. Punch in this code to enter an island of danger and combat, as prisoners and guards battle for control. Up to 50 players can join and when you're tasked as a prisoner, your mission is to escape and survive as a criminal in the city. You'll need to earn gold by making heists and robbing, then using the rewards to grab weapons and equipment.

PWR TINY TOWN 9683-4582-8184

Remember that Creative is not just about PvP games. It's also a place to enjoy fun or crazy experiences and Tiny Town ticks that box. Jump in for a real-life role-play fix and do stuff like buy a house, pick a job and save gold to select helpful items. With as many as 16 players allowed, you'll love the minigames at Tiny Town and taking on your opponents. A welcome break from a manic Battle Royale round!

GET CREATIVE

PANDVILL BOX FIGHTS 6562-8953-6567

Box fights are packed with tension and tactics. In a small-scale scrap where there's little room for errors or hiding, you and your squad mates go up against another outfit and the sharpest shooters will succeed. Pandvill Box Fights is 2v2 and with its decent loadout options, you'll want to sit high on the leaderboard and collect a good count of eliminations after all nine rounds. Best of Battle Royale luck to you!

ROCKETS VS CARS 2735-4519-3188

Being imaginative and coming up with an original idea will 'rocket' your map to new heights. Creator Bertbuilds has devised a simple but appealing Creative game, which sees you battle for the rockets or cars team. If you have the explosives at your fingertips, you must defend your platform from speedy attacks from vehicles. Switch to the cars and you raid ramps to knock players off. It's full-on, high-octane action.

5⁰ ZOMBIE INFECTION 5780-8881-5545

Great to play around Halloween, or any time that you want a Fortnite fright, this monster mash-up rewards bravery in bucketloads. The zombies are on a mission to track down and infect all the humans, while the humans just run and hide in the opposite direction. Use the speed boosts to zoom from the zombies and trade your bricks for helpful items.

CURSED SHORES 8V8 6760-9430-6957

Set around historic fortresses by the ocean, Cursed Shores 8v8 rode a wave of popularity in the combat ranking games throughout 2021. A team heads from their spawn point to hunt down the enemy, with a random set of parameters controlling each minigame. This could be having low gravity, starting with just 50 health and trying to get to a supply drop in the ocean. Clever use of vending machines becomes important.

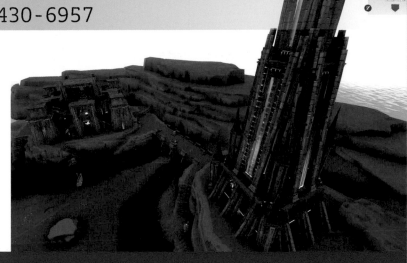

INFINITE LEVEL DEFAULT DEATH RUN 2368-2970-1351

Parkour powers at the ready! Forget how good or bad you are at weapon takedowns, because this is purely a test of your timing, running and jumping prowess. You work through a testing obstacle course, avoiding spike traps, setting off bouncers and landing in the right places. Creator Meep has even added car and boat levels for an awesome skills challenge. Remember to trigger the save points each time.

BREAKOUT: RESURRECTED 1495-3255-4588

Staying with the zombie theme, Breakout: Resurrected by TeamIdol is for up to four players who face waves of creepy creatures out to capture them. The creators keep updating the game with enhanced perks and awesome features such as speed boosts, instant weapon reloads and random mods like round skipping and double points mode. With crafting options and team revival tactics, there's much to think about in the quest to keep away from the gruesome ghouls!

WEAPONS GUIDE

Track the pros and cons of some of the greatest guns and weapons that have been available through Chapter 2. This is important info for taking control of any shootout.

SIDEWAYS RIFLE

Best For:

Only found in the Sideways zones, this powerful rifle shot straight to the top of weapon wishlists when it dropped in Chapter 2 Season 8, along with the other Sideways weapons.

- Fully auto with a speedy firing rate
- Damage multiplies when close to overheating
- DPS rate of 199.5 in mythic rarity

Best For:

SIDEWAYS MINIGUN

Load up with the new sideways minigun when you're in a squad shootout and your fellow players will smile ear to ear – it's awesome in team tussles!

- Get close to target to boost accuracy
- Available in uncommon to mythic
- Beware of cooldown

RAIL GUN

Making an explosive entrance in Chapter 2 Season 7, with its incredible ability to shoot through walls, some gamers loved the rail gun, while others thought it was too over-powered.

- Charge and beam function to focus on target
- Good in box fights
- No close-range scope

Best For:

Best For:

LEVER ACTION SHOTGUN

With a design that looks like a 20th century classic and only the second lever action to arrive, after the lever action rifle, this shottie should give you the confidence to excel in short-range battles.

- Good replacement for the pump shotgun
- Slower firing rate
- Can two-shot the enemy in rare to legendary variations

Best For:

SUPPRESSED ASSAULT RIFLE

In Chapter 2 Season 8, the suppressed assault rifle was obtainable by crafting a regular AR together with nuts and bolts. The bolt collecting was worth it for such a powerful stealthy option.

- Impressive all-round weapon
- Decent accuracy in mid to long-range
- Not heard if the enemy's at distance

BURST ASSAULT RIFLE

Can't choose between the suppressed and the burst AR? The burst can quickly knock down and eliminate your target and give you the power to press on!

- Suited to medium-range shooting
- Fires a devastating two-round burst
- Epic and legendary boast 140+ DPS

Best For:

AUTOMATIC SNIPER RIFLE

To take someone out from a safe distance, a sniper rifle is the best tool for the job. Just keep a steady hand and time your shots to perfection. This one can fire off shots quicker than most before a long reload.

- Uses medium ammunition
- Takes practice to use the scope and crosshair
- Reload time of nearly four seconds

Best For:

RAPID FIRE SMG

As well as looking mightily menacing, with its sleek matt black finish, this submachine gun will make quick work of enemies, though it absolutely tears through your supply of SMG ammunition.

- Magazine size 26 is small and needs constant reloading
- Shoot at speed
- As high as 250+ DPS at legendary rarity

Best For:

ROCKET LAUNCHER

Time to blow the opposition away and let them know who's bossing this battle! The rocket launcher is fun to use and frightening to be on the receiving end of.

- Legendary has structural damage of 330
- Players can hitch a ride on the rocket
- Be careful not to damage yourself upon launch

CHARGE SHOTGUN

Making its debut in Chapter 2 Season 3, the charge shotgun ranges from uncommon to legendary and should not be dismissed if you end up having it pointed in your direction.

- High damage in one-on-one short-range scraps
- Allow for charge time
- Can aim down sights and hip fire

Best For:

PISTOL

Probably the first weapon you'll find, but you'll likely want to ditch it for something better before long. However, it still has some decent benefits, including a good damage potential at all but the longest ranges.

- Strong all-rounder in early combat
- Good accuracy
- Can be used at targets further away

Best For:

Best For:

SUBMACHINE GUN

The humble submachine gun has been in and out of the vault for years, but when it's in play it gives players the advantage of speed, though it lacks effectiveness at range.

- Good substitute for a shotgun
- Useful for long-range too, but accuracy suffers
- Legendary reloads in under two seconds

35

BATTLE PASS

If you're a hardcore Fortnite player then you'll want to get involved with each season's Battle Pass. Take a tour to discover all about it.

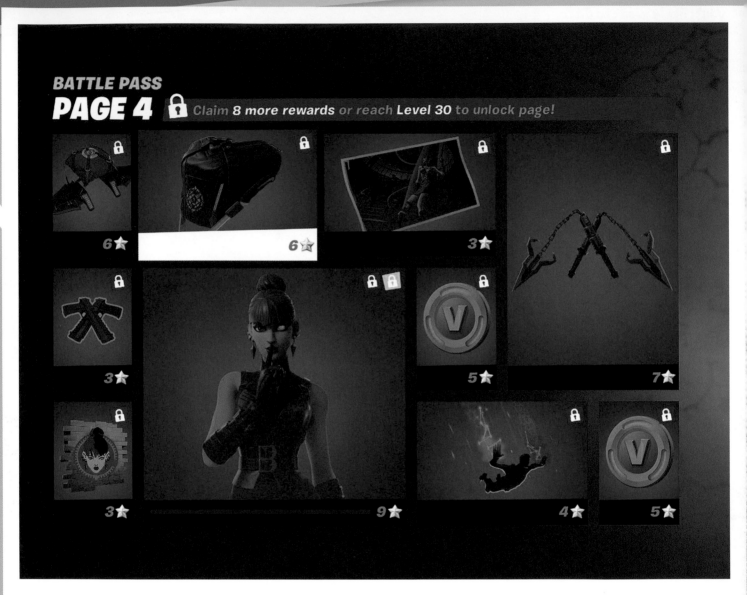

WHAT IS THE BATTLE PASS?

Costing 950 V Bucks, which is Fortnite's in-game currency, the Battle Pass gives gamers access to a seasonal challenge, where they can unlock exclusive cosmetics, earn extra V Bucks, pick up items and so much more, just by playing the game and earning experience points. Having the new Battle Pass each Season is not essential but is a nice bonus to your Fortnite experience.

HOW DOES IT WORK?

The Battle Pass is split into 100 tiers, which you advance to by gaining experience points playing in regular matches and completing special quests. As you pass each tier, you'll unlock a reward, such as special skins, emotes or icons that you can't get anywhere else. It will take a long time to unlock everything, but as it's open all Season-long, there should be plenty of opportunities to reach the end.

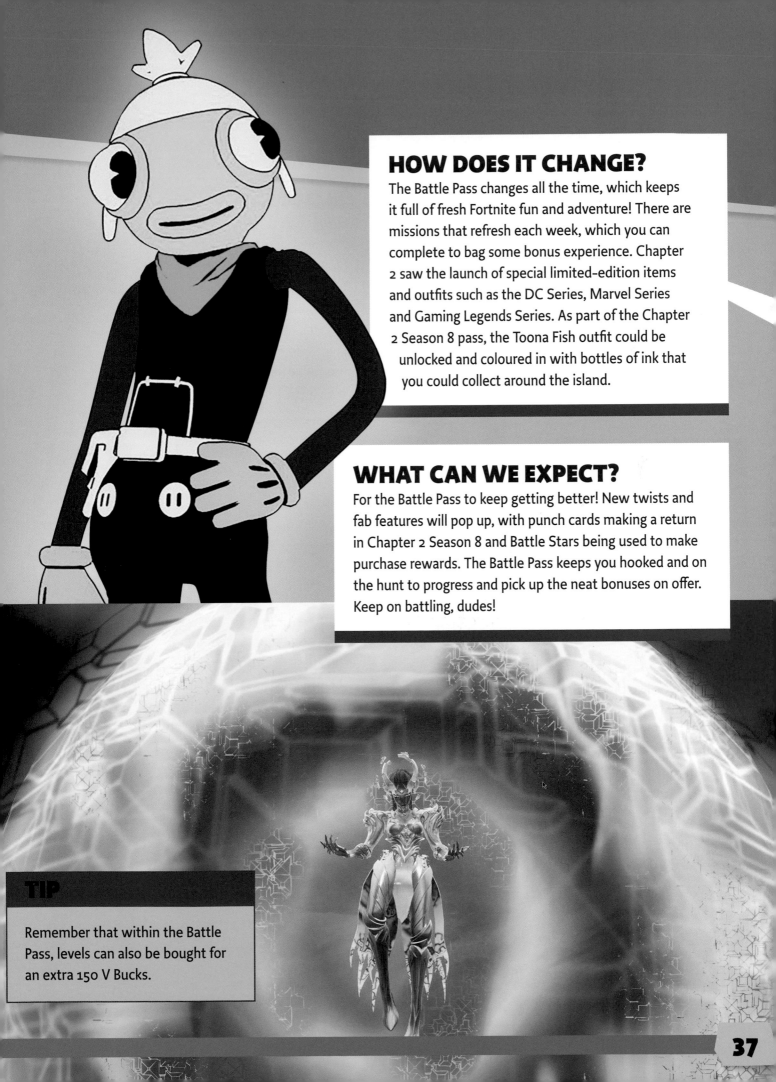

HOW DOES IT CHANGE?

The Battle Pass changes all the time, which keeps it full of fresh Fortnite fun and adventure! There are missions that refresh each week, which you can complete to bag some bonus experience. Chapter 2 saw the launch of special limited-edition items and outfits such as the DC Series, Marvel Series and Gaming Legends Series. As part of the Chapter 2 Season 8 pass, the Toona Fish outfit could be unlocked and coloured in with bottles of ink that you could collect around the island.

WHAT CAN WE EXPECT?

For the Battle Pass to keep getting better! New twists and fab features will pop up, with punch cards making a return in Chapter 2 Season 8 and Battle Stars being used to make purchase rewards. The Battle Pass keeps you hooked and on the hunt to progress and pick up the neat bonuses on offer. Keep on battling, dudes!

TIP

Remember that within the Battle Pass, levels can also be bought for an extra 150 V Bucks.

GET THE LOOK

Shooting, looting and building are vital aspects to bossing the battle, but if you haven't got the look, no one will give you a moment's notice! Scan this selection of hot Chapter 2 outfits ...

GRIMOIRE

It's never a good sign when your enemy is wearing a skull on their head, so beware of anyone sporting the epic Grimoire skin. This spooky lady was released in Chapter 2 Season 4 and has been scaring folks ever since.

FORTNITE FACT

The skin comes in two styles; one with the skull hood and one without.

BLOOM

Flower power rules Royale! As a reactive suit, Bloom sees subtle changes when damage is taken and there's always something to catch the eye in this Epic rarity outfit. When it rotates into the item shop, snap it up.

FORTNITE FACT

Bloom's Pluxarian Floraxe harvesting tool morphs onto the outfit's arm during use.

FABIO SPARKLEMANE

With a name like that, this outfit could hardly be plain and boring! Mr Sparklemane keeps the unicorn tradition alive in Fortnite and lights up even the darkest of combat situations. His gameplay-affecting ability makes him feared.

FORTNITE FACT

This 'fab' outfit comes in the Unicorn Flakes!!! set and comes in a variety of styles.

ORIN

Even though Orin first showed up in January 2021, his legacy survives among those Fortnite fans with a passion for manga-style skins. Regular item shop appearances have meant he's never far from dropping on the island.

FORTNITE FACT

Lexa is Orin's twin sister and both come from the Y-Labs Hunter Set.

WINDWALKER ECHO

The simple but strong and sophisticated style that the Windwalker Echo rocks says she's nothing but a serious Battle Royale contender. She has cool tattoos on her arm that will glow when she opens up the loot chests of the island!

FORTNITE FACT

She's one of the best uncommon outfits in Chapter 2, costing just 800 V-Bucks.

DYNAMO DANCER

Part of the Boundless set of 10 superhero skins, the legendary Dynamo Dancer is one of the most desirable skins in the game. You can customise every part of the outfit, including skin colour, hair, mask, suit pattern and colour, as well as whether her eyes are flaming or not!

FORTNITE FACT

Other Boundless heroes include Joltara, Backlash and the Mighty Volt.

J.B. CHIMPANSKI

Part monkey, part astronaut, part ... something else altogether?!
He became a popular outfit around the map in Chapter 2 Season 8 and whether he had his helmet on or off, J.B. Chimpanski always stood head and shoulders above other combat styles.

FORTNITE FACT

J.B. Chimpanski's exclusive built-in emote is the crazy Monkey Mosh routine.

BONEHEAD

Another skin, another skeleton – but at least this one doesn't look as menacing. The glowing eyes and cheeks suggest there's some sort of energy residing within its bones, so it could be a real force to be reckoned with on the battlefield.

FORTNITE FACT

Bonehead has its own back bling to match the blue energy of the outfit – the epic Back Burner.

TOONA FISH

This epic rarity outfit adds more than just a splash of colour. Toona Fish can be customised in quite some detail, from head colour to the hat, gloves, arms, legs, socks and shoes. Add the ink you think works best!

FORTNITE FACT

Toona Fish was also a character found on the Viking Vessel landmark during Chapter 2 Season 8.

JOY

If you had a spare 1,200 V Bucks burning a hole in your pocket during Chapter 2 Season 7, splashing it on Joy would bring you lots of, er ... joy! With a powerful rainbow design on her simple jeans and skates, she's a character who's proud to be different.

FORTNITE FACT

The Joy skin shows a condition called vitiligo, where pale patches appear on her skin.

TORIN

Unlocking cosmetics and spending nine Battle Stars during the Season 8 Battle Pass landed you with Torin. Epic Games call her "a hunter prepared for every dimension" and her matching back bling actually counts the eliminations she racks up!

FORTNITE FACT

Use the Sideways Shift emote to reveal her secondary style: Sideways Warrior.

KOR

Another Chapter 2 Season 8 Battle Pass skin, Kor comes from the Splinter Agent set and has more than a hint of stealthy assassin about her. The Trenchcoat selectable style is the one to opt for if you want to contrast her jet black dress with a splash of crimson red.

FORTNITE FACT

Kor is rumoured to have some suspicious links to the Imagined Order (IO) group.

MINTY BOMBER

This cool epic skin is fresh to death. Part of the Minty Legends set, she has a familiar tactical outfit with splashes of cool blue, a llama logo on her tee and piercing green eyes.

FORTNITE FACT

Other skins in the Minty Legends set include Fresh Aura and the bony Skellemint Oro.

CRZ-8

A futuristic verision of the amazing 8-Ball vs Scratch skin that came out at the start of Chapter 2, CRZ-8 has really grown up. The moody black cloak and digital 8-ball head will have you asking yourself if you're feeling lucky ...

FORTNITE FACT

Kondor's Zero Point style was unlocked at level 220 of the Season 5 Battle Pass.

THE DEVOURER

The sworn enemy of Mecha, The Devourer is a gigantic beast that has been sleeping under the island for years. But it's no longer trapped in its icy prison. He's a Frozen Series limited rarity, so he can only be purchased in the store in the Polar Legends pack.

FORTNITE FACT

The Devourer has a variant that dusts him in snow and has a giant castle tower on its back!

SPIRE IMMORTAL

Warning: sharp edges. Spire Immortal is a prickly customer, and if his sharp body armour doesn't hurt you, then his disturbing scowl will. It's an epic skin, which pairs perfectly with the Soul's Reach back bling.

FORTNITE FACT

There's a female variant skin available: Spire Assassin, which is much rarer than Immortal.

COOL COMBOS

Creating combinations of outfits with matching or well-suited back bling, harvesting tools and gliders is a special skill. How do you rate these clever combos?

CELESTE

PRISMABLADE

+

SPECTRAL STAR

AGENT JONESY

FLYCATCHER

+

PAPER PLANE

RAPSCALLION

STRONGBOX

+

STARRY FLIGHT

HEDRON

PICKAXIS

+

MULTIPOINT EDGE

HUSH

WEATHERED BLACK WRAP (ON AR)

+

SILENT STRIKE

LARS

SKY STRIPE

+

PROP CHOP

ROBOKEVIN

WHIRRR

+

POWER PICK

YUKI

SL1C3// D1C3

+

H4CK// P4CK

MO E C EATIVE CODE

DRIVERS VS SNIPERS 7467-1406-6184

With two teams and as many as 16 players involved, this is a head-to-head meeting as vehicles and weapons scrap for supremacy. Similar to the Rockets vs Cars Creative game, but this time rifles and other weapons are in play and you can run and explore on the ground if you come out of the vehicle. As a sniper up on the target bridge, just dodge the cars and shoot away as you tackle the five rounds.

OUTLAST (FORTNITE EDITION) 8752-7425-3922

Creator IFrost Origins said it took him over two months to lay down this mega map in Creative, and once you play for a while you can see why it took that long. Outlast is a an awesome single player horror-based game where you must follow instructions, search for clues and items and complete missions, while all the time be ready for a shock attack from creatures. The music, the darkness and the suspense is sooo cool!

CYBER STADIUM 6199-8972-3700

A neon-inspired outfit like Luminos or DJ Yonder would be perfect for this punky game. It's set in a futuristic stadium scene where teams battle and race around to eliminate each other, capture the opposing flag and hunt for items and upgrade opportunities. Matches are short and frantic and keep looking high and low for danger, while making the most of any boosts you can.

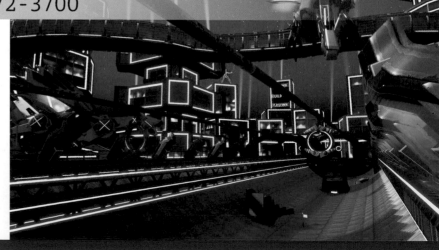

COLOR SPLASH 3060-5550-3213

Often the most simple Fortnite Creative maps can be the most playable. Color Splash is a fun and straightforward challenge where teams compete to spread their side's colour across the map. The difficulty is that both teams have weapons and are not that keen on just letting each other paint as they please! The weapon loadouts will alter occasionally and there are enough variations to keep the mechanics fresh and interesting.

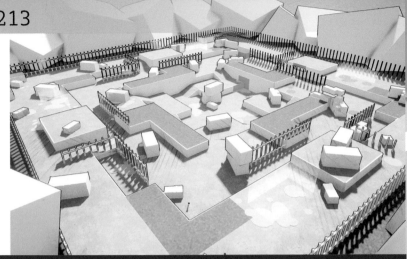

FORTNITE BASKETBALL 3613-5135-9180

You don't have to be a court star and a complete baller to get hooked on Skttlz's fun Fortnite Basketball minigame. For starters, the basketball is replaced by fish (weird, huh?!) and you get two points for successfully throwing it through the hoop. There's space for as many as ten players and you'll be on the blue or green team. If you want to play defence, six decent swipes with your pickaxe will eliminate your opponent.

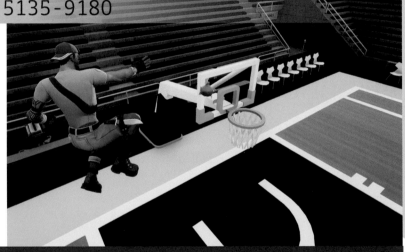

DEMOLITION DERBY 6585-2275-1515

Creator Ritual must be a big lover of vehicles and chaos, because that pretty much sums up Demolition Derby. The idea is just to ram and slam through ten tense rounds of metal-bashing madness. Drive your motor around the stadium, building speed so you can crunch cars and smash their health and shield. Just like in regular Battle Royale, the storm will shrink so your driving space becomes smaller and scarier!

ITEMS CHECKLIST

Always keep an eye on the items appearing around the island. Here are some slick suggestions that will give you a head start over your battleground opponents.

HARPOON GUN

'Miscellaneous' means the harpoon gun can perform several cool missions during its use before the ten charges have been fired. Acting as a weapon and a fishing tool, the pointy harpoon can be fired at opponents to drag them close to you and it will also deal damage to a structure it smashes into. Fans were pleased to see it return during Chapter 2 Season 8.

ITEM TYPE:
Miscellaneous

ITEM TYPE:
Healing

CHILI CHUG SPLASH

A spicy addition in Chapter 2 Season 8, this upgrade on the regular chug splash has a few fancy benefits. Firstly, chili chug splash acts as a squad booster by beefing up your health by 20. It just needs to be thrown and players caught in its radius, including enemy players, get the benefit. It also provides a speed enhancement for around a minute.

TIP

Chili chug splash could be collected for 210 bars from The Brat character, but was also dropped by supply llamas.

SHADOW STONE

ITEM TYPE:
Foraged

Other types of foraged items found in Fortnite include Zero Point crystals, hop rocks and common vegetables. Shadow stones, which returned in Chapter 2 Season 8, are different to all of these because when they are consumed you literally became a shadow of your former self! Unleash one of these and for 45 seconds you become a purple haze that's bursting with speed and very tricky for others to spot. Super sneaky.

SHADOW FLOPPER

ITEM TYPE:
Healing

The rare consumable shadow flopper is a fish worth waiting for as you cast your rod in the water. Ranging in size and colour, from orange to blue and green, it'll perk you up to the tune of 40 HP. Plus, consuming one of these tasty treats gives you the same effect as the mysterious shadow stone.

MOUNTED TURRET

ITEM TYPE:
Trap

That's right, the mounted turret is technically classed as an item and not a weapon. It debuted way back in the original Season 6, but saw a return in Chapter 2. Via turret donation boards, players donated bars so that these deadly damage dealers cropped up in various spots around the map. Jumping on one of these is a thrill not to be missed!

ITEM TYPE:
Trap

ARMORED WALL

Think that a standard wall doesn't offer enough protection from weapon attacks? No problem – stick an armored wall down with it to max out your defences! This top trap item dropped during Chapter 2 and was an instant hit with pro builders and newbies alike. It must be added to a wall already built or configured so that it's automatically placed when you lay down a structure. They first appeared in supply drops and Epic Games have said that the walls are "ultra protective."

TIP

You can't edit an armored wall, so think about their placement before you get into a shootout.

ITEM TYPE:
Miscellaneous

RECON SCANNER

Some Fortnite fans reckon the recon scanner is actually a slow-moving projectile weapon, but any damage its scans deal to players is very minimal. Instead, this item's purpose is to survey an area from a safe distance and highlight the enemy players and chests hidden within. The scanner searches an area using recon bolts and it stays highlighted for 15 seconds.

FORTNITE FRIENDZY

This was a unique way for you and your Battle Royale buddies to pick up some extra awesome items and rewards during Chapter 2. Fortnite Friendzy worked by giving you points for the amount of time you played together. You just needed to register through the official Epic Games system. Rewards on offer included the Aquari-Axe pickaxe, Life's a Beach wrap and Outer Space handshake emoticon.

DANCE OFF

Get your dancing gear on! Whether they appear through the Battle Pass, item shop or as special gifts and rewards, emotes always get gamers grooving and moving.

BUILD UP

Get your dancing shoes on for Build Up, a hip-shaking, arm-waving emote that looks super cute. The perfect dance to lull enemies into a trap.

EVERYBODY LOVES ME

Perfect for conveying your confidence on the battlefield, Everybody Loves Me is a love letter to yourself ... from yourself. Why not?

DON'T START NOW

Make sure you're well-hidden for this emote, because it's a long one. The sassy shoulder wiggles and jerking knee moves will get you puffing.

JAMBOREE

If your prefer an emote that looks like an uncle at a wedding, this hopping, arm-swinging number will be your go-to move on the island.

ELECTRO SWING

It's all in the legs! Get your toes and heels tapping to the rhythm and your arms will have no choice but to swing along. Old school.

PHONE IT IN

Where did that saxophone come from? What else is your skin hiding from you. Take a deep breath, then unleash a super sax solo.

ROCK PAPER SCISSORS

Sure you could settle the Battle Royale with all this new-fangled weapons, but how about a good old game of RPS to decide the victor?

EXTRA TERRESTRIAL

If your Fortnite skills are out of this world then show it with this mind-boggling ballet of the arms and hands. Perfect for a sci-fi skin.

SHANTY FOR A SQUAD

Shanties have enjoyed a resurgence in recent years, so get it on the action with ANOTHER hidden instrument and bang your drum.

WATERWORKS

Let's be honest, most games won't go exactly how you plan, but it's okay to just let it all out and have a good cry. Especially if you have the Waterworks emote!

FIND THE IMPOSTOR

It's a battle of agents versus impostors in the sneaky Impostors game mode. Discover all you need to know about this epic espionage environment.

TIP

When the Impostors mode came out, Epic Games also ran a ten-day minigame called Impostors Trials with up to five million players able to register!

THE BRIDGE BATTLE

Devised for between 4 and 10 players, with 10 being preferable as it leads to more exciting and puzzling gameplay, Impostor is set on a submarine called The Bridge. Two impostors will be randomly chosen (or just one if there are less than 8 people) and their job is to eliminate the agents and seize control of the sub before they're discovered as the saboteurs. Agents must complete assignments to keep The Bridge in working order for as long as it takes to unveil the impostors.

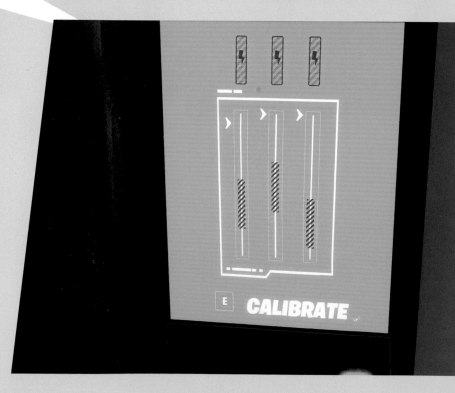

COMPLETE ASSIGNMENTS
BEWARE THE 2 IMPOSTORS!

E CALIBRATE

ASSIGNMENT ANALYSIS

As well as agents needing to do the assignments to keep The Bridge functioning, evil impostors also share the work that's detailed in a common list. Doing these will hopefully earn the (misplaced) trust of the rest of the gang. But, when the impostors help with assignments they are also edging the agents nearer to completing their objective and reaching victory. It's a fine line of blending in without helping too much.

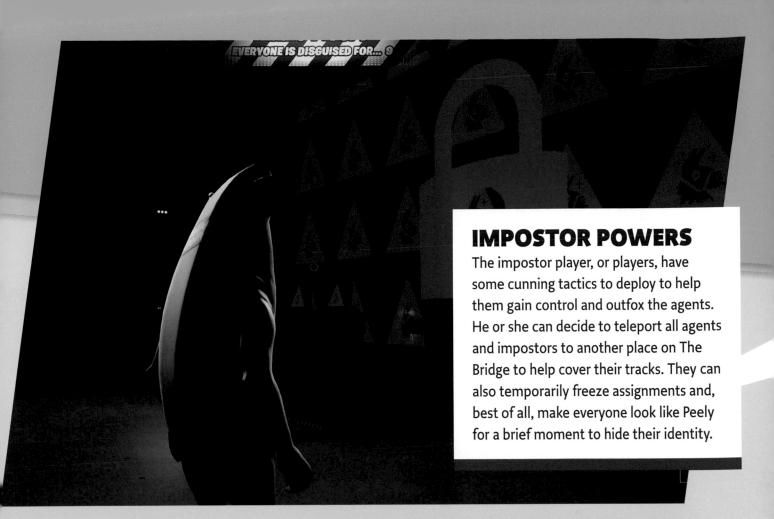

IMPOSTOR POWERS

The impostor player, or players, have some cunning tactics to deploy to help them gain control and outfox the agents. He or she can decide to teleport all agents and impostors to another place on The Bridge to help cover their tracks. They can also temporarily freeze assignments and, best of all, make everyone look like Peely for a brief moment to hide their identity.

DEADLY DISCUSSION

Triggering the discussion panel in the submarine's centre room or after you have found an eliminated agent can trigger a discussion. During discussions, agents and impostors exchange info via the quick chat menu or emotes. This can point the finger at who people think is the impostor. The discussion ends in a vote – now's your chance to decide who the bad dude is!

WE LOVE LTMs!

As well as the special Impostors mode, Limited Time Modes (LTMs) remain a popular feature throughout Chapter 2.

COSMIC SUMMER

You can be guaranteed that when the weather gets warmer outside and the sun beats down, the action on the island starts to heat up too! Packed with sizzlin' summer surprises, the Cosmic Summer event ran during the summer months and saw the return of LTMs such as Pro 100, Freak Flights Air Royale and Bios Zone Wars Trio. As well as these hot releases, new and returning summery outfits shone under the dazzling sun, including Midsummer Midas, Scuba Crystal, Summer Drift, Unpeely and Beach Brutus.

SHOCKWAVE

Get ready for a shock to the system with the Shockwave Limited Time Mode. This has popped up throughout Chapter 2 and the basic principle is that each hit with a weapon will knock a player backwards. Keep hitting an opponent and eventually you could push them beyond the storm wall where they'll begin to take damage. You'll need to safely steer yourself through three frantic Shockwave rounds to claim a Victory Royale.

ISLAND GAMES

The Fortnite fun continued in Island Games, a timed event in which a bunch of Creative LTMs became the focus. The impressive Creative maps that were featured included Prison Breakout, Wildlands, Red vs Blue Lava and Finest Realistic. Each LTM boasted three special quests to tick off, which helped towards unlocking great rewards in the event, from a range of thematic wraps, pickaxes, banners and emoticons.

SPRING BREAKOUT

In 2021, Spring Breakout was Fortnite's first ever spring and Easter-themed event and it was packed with 'eggcellent' ideas, in-game rewards and exciting outfits. Spring Breakout Cup was a duos mode where you and a teammate could earn points during a three-hour event. The egg launcher item also showed up as an explosive extra and the fan fave skins of Bunny Brawler, Rabbit Raider and Quackling appeared in the Item Shop.

ROYALE RIDES

Keep on track with what's moving around the island thanks to this rapid rundown of some of the most memorable vehicles from Chapter 2.

SAUCERS

Sadly, saucers were vaulted in Chapter 2 Season 8, but for a while they took the vehicle experience to another planet ... sort of. This alien creation was capable of zooming you and your squad across the map, firing at landlubber enemies along the way. It even had the ability to abduct players and objects from the ground below. The speed boost was a cool feature too.

TIP

Watch out for more special edition motors speeding into Fortnite. In Chapter 2 Season 7, the flashy Ferrari 296 GTB arrived and got fans racing behind the wheel.

100% UNOFFICIAL

CAR-NAGE

Cars revved into action back in Chapter 2 Season 3 and have been a mechanical mainstay during combat ever since. Their main role is to whisk you away from an attack, evade the storm or cause damage to opponents and buildings. The Whiplash sports car is the speediest of the bunch, while the OG Bear pickup and Mudflap trucks are hulking beasts with more HP to withstand weapons and collisions.

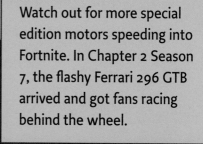

IO VEHICLES

These black beauties rocked up in Chapter 2 Season 7, as variants of the standard cars and trucks. Jumping into the colossal cab of the Imagined Order truck and putting your foot down meant you could crash through just about any structure in your path. Just be careful of the fuel range though, as in normal mode all cars need juice in the tank and it will deplete the more you drive.

OFF-ROAD TYRES

Vehicle mods and mash-ups get a big thumbs up from Fortnite motoring fans. Chunky, oversized off-road tyres were a bit of a game changer as your vehicle could suddenly tackle tough terrain and climb gradients that were previously out of bounds. Off-road tyres were stashed as floor loot around the map and next to gas stations. All you had to do to trick out your ride was launch the collected items at your vehicle and voila!

MOTORBOATS

Don't forget the humble motorboat, which added a totally new form of travel at the beginning of Chapter 2. Since their introduction, they have seen a few changes through the seasons and now require fuel before you can cruise the canals of the island, but their missile launch and ability to move over land for a short time makes them a top transport tool.

OPEN THE VAULT

What's in and what's out? Items and weapons are placed in the vault throughout each season, so check out some stuff that's either appeared or disappeared.

PROP-IFIER

Perhaps the coolest item to drop during the alien-infested Chapter 2 Season 7, the prop-ifier properly fooled your enemy! It was a tool that blended you in with your surroundings; it gave you a list of prop items you could become, and you did just that when you activated it. Then, you could transform back to normal and wipe out your opponent or stay hidden to evade danger. Such a shame when it was vaulted!

VAULTED

TIP

When you're hidden as a prop item you can still move around, but be careful as this will give your identity away.

INFLATE-A-BULL

This was a one-season wonder that appeared only during Chapter 2 Season 7, but what a wondrous and popular item it became. With the inflate-a-bull strapped to your back, it just needed to be blown up and you would be wrapped in its big and bouncy shield and could bounce, glide and float from danger. Rolling along inside this giant suit would see you escape danger, although it could be popped open with enemy shots.

UNVAULTED

BOUNCER

During the Flying High Week, which was one of the attractions of the Wild Weeks events, plenty of cool things made a return from the vault. The bouncer trap item was one of those that had been dormant for a while and players were reminded of its powers in springing you upwards and then scrubbing off the fall damage once gravity kicked in. The rift-to-go and launch pad were also unvaulted at the same time.

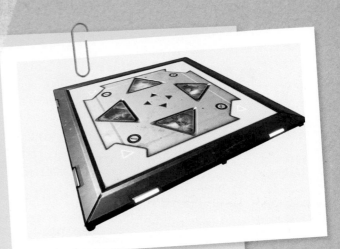

UNVAULTED

TOP SECRET

SUPPRESSED SNIPER RIFLE

Unfortunately the suppressed sniper rifle has been in and out of the vault so often, players never really have time to adjust to using it, or combatting someone else who is using it. When it is in play, this powerful weapon is a master of blasting long-range targets with its high degree of accuracy and DPS score of 33 in legendary form.

VAULTED

PLASMA CANNON

Making a brief appearance in Chapter 2 Season 7 before being thrown in the vault the following season, the Imagined Order-inspired plasma cannon was described as a "science lesson gone wrong" by Epic Games. It certainly did the right thing for players using it, though, as the plasma balls unleashed an electrical dome of energy that smashed building and opponents in its wake. The plasma cannon could be crafted as well as being found in loot, but was maybe a tad too strong.

VAULTED

TOP SECRET

SCOPED ASSAULT RIFLE

The scoped AR popped in and out of the island throughout Chapter 2. Gamers miss its excellent accuracy and power from range when the weapon goes missing from their loadout options. The sniper rifle is the next best choice, but it doesn't have the high fire rate or short reloads that and assault rifle enjoys. When the scoped AR next gets another run out, it'll surely be a popular choice once again.

UNVAULTED

SLONE'S BURST ASSAULT RIFLE

The standard burst AR was unlocked at times during Chapter 2, but let's take a moment to focus briefly on the special Slone's burst assault rifle. It is a powerful mythic variant and at first could only be acquired by defeating the Doctor Slone character. With a damage per second score of 178, it was more powerful than almost any other AR that had been put in the hands of battlers!

UNVAULTED

TIP

The plasma cannon has five charges, so they should be used wisely before the weapon disappears when it is exhausted.

ALIEN NANITES

Alien nanites had a double purpose. Lay down this throwable item and a large anti-gravity field was whipped up, creating a zone for 30 seconds where players could zoom in any direction and become a hard target to hit. Gravity had a minimal effect while in the zone. Alien nanites could also be used as a crafting ingredient to make some awesome weapons.

VAULTED

MORE CREATIVE CODES

FORTNITE MURDER MYSTERY 8864-2994-8489

Fortnite riffed so much on their own version of Among Us through 2021, with cool spy and hunter themes, and this Creative adds yet another twist to the copycat saga. The setting is a forest lodge with lots of floors and as the detective, your job is to eliminate the killer and protect the others. Doing tasks, like watering plants and buying books, rewards you with gold to buy items. Watch out for the bad guy on the prowl and if you want time out, there's even a flashy dance floor!

PARKING SIMULATOR 1982-2979-6294

Zen Creative hit upon a cool idea with this fun Fortnite map. Coming under the casual, puzzle and race tags, your task is to navigate your vehicle through 12 rounds and park your way to victory. Yes, it's literally just parking your car. However, it's packed with weekly challenges and updates too, so it never gets boring. You need to slide and guide through the zones and manoeuvre your machine into the perfect parking spot. Precision driving at its best!

GIANT GIFTS HIDE AND SEEK 3837-4047-8371

There's a heavy Christmas theme going on, but that doesn't mean Giant Gifts is not playable all-year round. At the start of each game, one seeker will be secretly selected and then the other hiders have 30 seconds to search for a spot to hide among the huge objects. Rounds last for seven minutes and if you're captured, you then join the seeker team. Run and hide in this frantic Fortnite experience.

DEFEND THE KING 7860-3454-9163

Forget Battle Royale – this is a proper fight to earn 'royal' respect! Designed for a minimum of four players, you'll be given a bunch of upgradeable spells along with the typical arsenal of weaponry. The aim of the game is to protect the king and defend your castle tower with honour. But the world is a little bit more unforgiving than normal, with lethal lava everywhere and danger lurking in the dark, so this minigame requires complete focus and quick thinking.

MALL MANIA 1896-0780-3687

A spectacular shopping mall setting mashed up with manic gunfights – it's time to mix retail with royale and scrap to be the rulers of the complex. Released by Itz Earthy in early 2021, Mall Mania attracts fans of capture the point games, as it sees you and your team plan to control zones and pick up franchise points. The zone rotates every two minutes, so you can't get too comfortable for too long and there's always a new approach needed to your fighting tactics.

THE CURSE OF JONESY 8530-7928-4892

We all love Jonesy - he's one of the most recognisable faces in the whole of Fortnite, and here your quest is to do what it takes to defeat the curse of Jonesy! With a parkour, escape-style theme to this map, the aim is to take on and master the four trials, collecting crucial crystals from each to finally break the cruel curse. Huge water zones, bridges and obstacles populate this stunning setting.

FORTNITE QUIZ

The next four pages are full of Fortnite quiz questions that will test your knowledge of Battle Royale. How many correct answers will you get?

4 Who is this character?

A. Nurse Smith   B. Doctor Slone   C. Surgeon Jones

1 What's the in-game Fortnite competition where gamers are challenged to capture the best images?

A. Fortography   B. Battle Picto-Royale   C. Image Order

5 How many seasons were there in Chapter 1?

A. 9   B. 10   C. 20

2 Which of these is not a genuine series of outfits?

A. Icon Series   B. Slurp Series   C. Master Series

6 What nickname has the Cube been given?

A. Kevin   B. Kalvin   C. Keith

3 In weaponry, what does ADS stand for?

A. Always detect strangers   B. Aim dead straight   C. Aim down sights

7 Spectral spine, hard case hero and lil' black heart are types of what?

A. Location   B. Back Bling   C. Weapon

8 The 'War Effort' is a phrase used in the storyline of which season?

A. Chapter 1 Season X

B. Chapter 2 Season 5

C. Chapter 2 Season 8

9 What date does Fortnite celebrate its birthday?

A. 24 September

B. 1 January

C. 29 February

10 When the sporty kickoff set launched in 2021, how many football clubs were involved?

A. 3

B. 10

C. 23

11 'Force Written' is an anagram of which Fortnite service?

A. Fortnite Creative

B. Fortnite Crew

C. Fortnite Cosplay

12 What type of ammo does a submachine gun use?

A. Awesome ammo

B. Heavy ammo

C. Light ammo

14 This is the outline of which Chapter 2 outfit?

A. Guggimon

B. Joy

C. Grimey

15 What does the abbreviation POI actually mean?

A. Point of interest

B. Position of interest

C. Power on iPhone

13 Whereabouts on the map is Holly Hedges found?

A. North

B. East

C. West

16 In which season did The Mothership arrive?

A. Chapter 2 Season 7

B. Chapter 2 Season 1

C. Season 1

17 What's the name of this colourful outfit?

A. Summer Skye

B. Cuddle Team Leader

C. Fabio Sparklemane

18 This voting device, from Chapter 2 Season 8, was called a what?

A. Donation board

B. Voting station

C. Notice board

19 Which of these outfits appeared first in Battle Royale?

A. Chomp Sr.

B. Double Agent Wildcard

C. Harry Kane

21 Which superstar was part of the Fortnite Rift Tour?

A. Drake

B. Ariana Grande

C. Ed Sheeran

20 What is Fortnite's other 'player v environment' mode called?

A. Defeat The World

B. Rule The World

C. Save The World

22 The new feature that lets wraps appear on outfits, pickaxes and back blings was called what?

A. Wrappables

B. Wearables

C. Fluffybles

23 How long does a cozy campfire burn for?

A. 10 Seconds

B. 25 Seconds

C. 60 Seconds

21
What colour are bars?

A. Silver   B. Rainbow Colours   C. Gold

22
Can you name this exciting exotic weapon?

A. Boom sniper rifle   B. Bolt action sniper rifle   C. Storm scout

27
Agent Peely comes from which set?

A. Banana Royale   B. Banana Bunch   C. Banana Ice Cream

23
What colour is associated with epic rarity weapons?

A. Green   B. Blue   C. Purple

29
Which of these is NOT a genuine emote?

A. Good Guy   B. Gotcha   C. Gloss

30
How many people can ride inside the mudflap truck?

A. 2   B. 4   C. 5

25
Put a location name to this image.

A. Misty Meadows   B. Retail Row   C. Weeping Woods

BACK LATER, FOLKS!

This is the end of our Fortnite flashback and gameplay guide, but remember that the fight for Victory Royale is relentless. Fortnite is continually changing, updating, improving and expanding. Who knows what will happen next on the island? The only thing you can be assured of is that you won't want to miss a moment of the action.

Keep loading up, keep dropping from the Battle Bus and keep learning what it takes to be the best that you can. Whether you enjoy solo scraps, duo attacks or full-on squad raids, make sure you always have fun the moment your boots hit the ground. That's what Fortnite's No.1 target has always been – to entertain the millions of fans who come back game after game, season after season and year after year.

Until next time, never rest for a second as the Battle Royale rages.

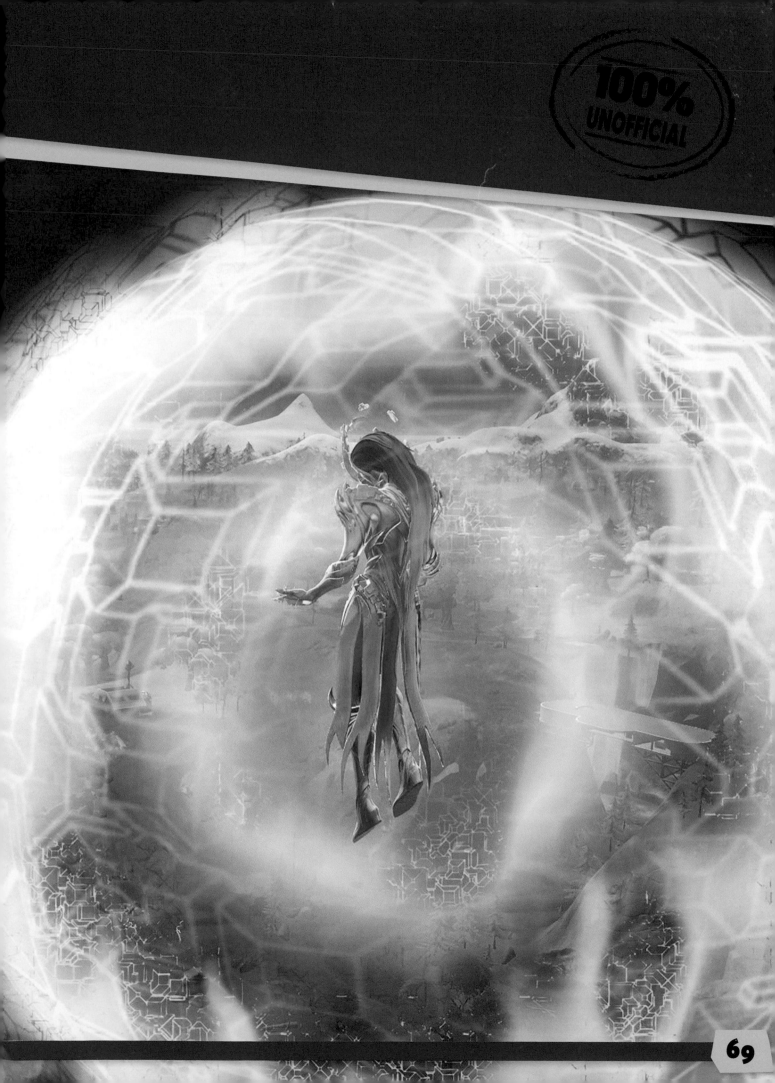